GIANTS OF THE DEEP

Arianemetera

Written by
Q. L. Pearce

Illustrated by
Steven James Petruccio

CHECKERBOARD PRESS

NEW YORK

To Ethie, for always being there
—Q.L.P.

To my wife KathyAnn and my daughter Stephanie
—S.J.P.

Acknowledgment

*I would like to express my thanks to Rimmon Fay, Ph.D.,
director of the Pacific Bio-Marine Laboratory, Venice, California,
for his careful review of the manuscript and illustrations.*
—Q.L.P.

Published by Checkerboard Press, Inc.
30 Vesey Street, New York, NY 10007

CONTENTS

The Sea—A Realm of Giants...8

The Blue Whale 10-11

The Sperm Whale *and* The Giant Squid..................................12-13

The Giant Manta Ray *and* The Ocean Sunfish.......................14-15

The Hammerhead Shark *and* The Great White Shark...........16-17

The Great Barracuda *and* The Giant Starfish.......................18-19

The Oarfish *and* The Swordfish..20-21

The Leatherback Turtle *and* The Bluefin Tuna.......................22-23

The Lion's Mane Jellyfish *and* The Walrus...........................24-25

The Humpback Whale *and* The Gray Whale.........................26-27

The Whale Shark *and* The Megamouth Shark 28-29

The Blue Marlin *and* The Sailfish..30-31

The Killer Whale *and* The Leopard Seal 32-33

The Elephant Seal *and* The Emperor Penguin 34-35

The Great Barrier Reef...36-37

The Giant Clam *and* The Yellow Sea Snake...........................38-39

The Pacific Jewfish *and* The Australian Trumpet 40-41

The Japanese Spider Crab *and* The Giant Sea Anemone........42-43

The Electric Eel *and* The Arapaima 44-45

THE SEA—A REALM OF GIANTS

The largest living animal, perhaps the largest animal that has ever lived, is the incredible blue whale, and it is just one of the many giants that swim in the Earth's seas. Huge whales glide through every ocean, gigantic sharks prowl silently through their watery realm, and immense squid dwell in the depths. And all of these animals are larger than the largest land animal, the African elephant.

How are these oceangoing supergiants able to reach such proportions? One important key to the riddle is gravity. Land animals are generally limited by the weight that their legs can bear. But in the sea, the salty ocean water buoys an animal up, setting it free from many of the restrictions of gravity that affect land dwellers. In fact, a modern whale could not survive for long onshore. Although it is an air breather, its extraordinary weight would prevent it from easily drawing a breath. As if that weren't enough, the creature would soon overheat because of its thick layer of blubber and its heat-conserving size (large animals lose body heat more slowly than smaller creatures).

But not all giants in the ocean are of gigantic size—not as compared to humans, that is. The giant clam, for instance, is just big enough for an average eight-year-old child to crouch comfortably inside, but compared to other, much smaller clams, it is huge indeed. Whether or not an animal can be called a "giant" depends on the usual size of animals similar to it. Moreover, within a given "giant" species, some individuals may grow well beyond the average size of their fellows. These are the record holders, and you will discover many of them in this book.

Why are some ocean animals giants? Since animals grow no larger than the size that is best suited to their survival, and since there are so many large creatures in the ocean, great size must in some ways be very beneficial. And it is. For one thing, large size protects many otherwise defenseless creatures from predators. A blue whale calf may fall prey to sharks, but with the exception of humans, healthy adult whales have few enemies. Large size can also be useful to a predator such as the great white shark, since it enables the shark to hunt and capture more and bigger prey. Smaller ocean giants, such as the giant crab, also can dominate their particular environment because of their large size.

Giants are found in all of Earth's oceans, from the steamy tropics to the polar seas. As you read this book, you will meet many animals that not only share a similar region or habitat, but also, in one way or another, depend on large size for their survival. Perhaps somewhere, far below the surface, an undiscovered behemoth lurks in the inky depths. It's certainly possible, because the sea is not only a realm of giants—it is also Earth's last great realm of mystery.

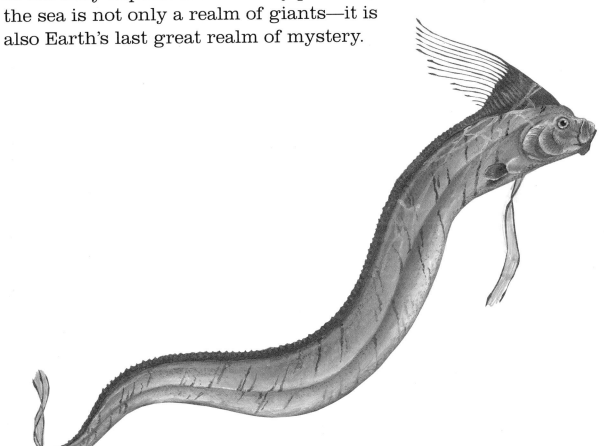

THE BLUE WHALE

THE LARGEST LIVING ANIMAL ON LAND OR IN THE SEA IS THE 80- TO 90-FOOT-long blue whale. With a heart that alone can weigh 8,000 pounds and a tongue that can weigh nearly 2,000 pounds, this creature's average weight is an astounding 280,000 pounds. Newborn blue whales are record setters, too. Like most other mammals, the blue whale calf begins as a barely visible egg in its mother's body. But by the time the baby is born, it is 25 feet long and weighs up to 6,000 pounds. On a rich diet of about 600 quarts of milk each day, the young calf *doubles* its birth weight in just one week.

Record Holder

Female blue whales are generally larger than males. The longest female blue whale ever measured was 110 feet, 2 inches long. She may have been the heftiest, too, but her weight was not recorded. Another huge female was a little more than 90 feet long and weighed in at 374,000 pounds.

You might think that a creature as gigantic as the blue whale would feed on some of the largest fish in the sea, but actually it feeds on one of the smallest—a tiny shrimp called krill. The whale uses its baleen (buh-LEEN) to strain the krill from seawater. Baleen is the tough material that grows in fringes from the animal's upper jaw. The 40-inch-long, 2½-foot-wide fringes form a kind of filter that allows water to escape but traps the krill. A blue whale may eat 8,000 pounds of krill each day. To eat a similar amount in spaghetti, you would have to gobble down about 16,000 servings every 24 hours.

THE SPERM WHALE

T HIS SEA MAMMAL REALLY "USES ITS HEAD"! IN FACT, THE SPERM WHALE'S head makes up about one-quarter of the creature's 60-foot length. Its head contains a reservoir of waxy material called spermaceti (sper-muh-SEET-ee), which may help to make the animal buoyant. That could come in handy to a whale that weighs somewhere between 70,000 and 100,000 pounds! Although the sperm whale is much smaller than the blue whale, it pursues much larger prey than does that gentle giant. Typically, the sperm whale hunts for giant squid, sharks, and other large fish. Up to 30 pairs of teeth stud the sperm whale's slim lower jaw. At up to 8 inches long, these cone-shaped teeth are the largest in any known animal. This whale can also claim to have the world's largest brain, which weighs a whopping 20 pounds—about six times more than a human brain.

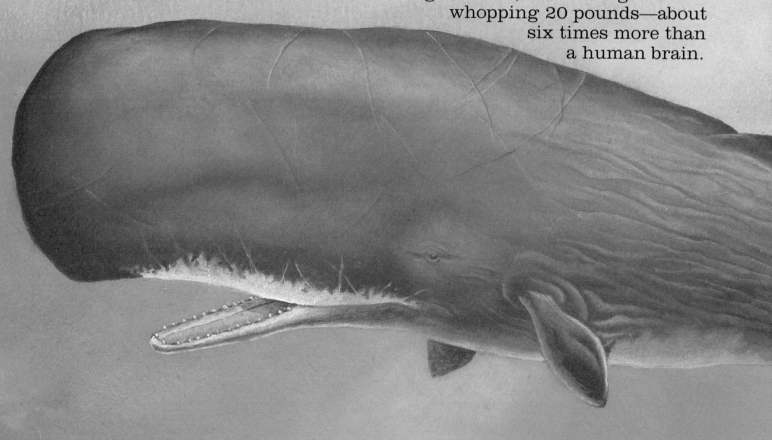

Record Holder

The largest sperm whale on record was a male nearly 68 feet long, weighing 144,000 pounds.

THE GIANT SQUID

THE FAVORITE FOOD OF THE SPERM WHALE IS THE BOTTOM-DWELLING GIANT squid, which can grow up to 55 feet long and weigh about 5,000 pounds. The huge squid has two wiry tentacles as well as eight arms lined with sucker disks for grasping prey. Each disk is nearly 2 inches wide. Since there have been no reported sightings of a living giant squid, most of what we know about this animal has been learned from studying remains washed up onshore. We can be certain, though, that sperm whales prey upon the mysterious beasts because some captured whales have displayed deep scars on their hides left by squid suckers.

Record Holder

The giant squid is thought to have the largest eyes of any animal on Earth. They can measure anywhere from 9 to 15 inches across. The human eye, by contrast, averages a mere one inch across!

THE GIANT MANTA RAY

T HE LARGEST MEMBER OF THE RAY FAMILY, THE 3,000-POUND GIANT MANTA ray seems to fly through the sea on huge wings. These "wings" are actually fins that may be as wide as 23 feet across from fin to fin. The 17-foot-long giant manta ray is also known as the devil ray because it appears to have horns protruding from its head. In fact, these "horns" are actually two rolled-up fins that the animal can unroll. When the paddle-shaped fins are fully extended, the giant manta ray uses them to guide plankton (tiny floating plants and sea creatures) and small fish into its wide mouth.

Fun Fact

On rare occasions, a female manta ray may give birth to her young during a spectacular leap out of the water. That makes the manta ray the only fish that can give birth in midair!

THE OCEAN SUNFISH

THE OCEAN SUNFISH LOOKS LIKE A HUGE, SCALELESS FISH HEAD WITH A PAIR of tall curious fins. Instead of ending in a tail, its body ends in a wide sort of ruffle, called a clavus (CLAY-vus). This strange, slow-swimming animal is usually 5 to 6 feet in length, and its fins may stretch 8 feet from tip to tip. An average weight of about 2,000 pounds qualifies the ocean sunfish as the world's heaviest bony fish. (A bony fish has bones instead of cartilage for support. Sharks and rays are examples of fish that have cartilage.) The sunfish is also the champion egg producer: One captured female contained 300 million tiny eggs! Newly hatched young look nothing like their parents—only about an eighth of an inch long, the round, spiny little fish are complete with tails.

Record Holder

The largest ocean sunfish ever reported was discovered in Australian waters. It measured 13 feet long and 14 feet from fin tip to fin tip, and it weighed a staggering 5,017 pounds.

THE HAMMERHEAD SHARK

WITH ITS BIZARRE HAMMER-SHAPED HEAD THAT SETS IT APART FROM OTHER sea creatures, it's easy to see how the 1,000-pound great hammerhead shark got its name. Commonly reaching 12 feet in length, this shark has eyes and nostrils at the outer tips of the "hammer," which may be up to 3 feet across. The great hammerhead shark usually feeds on fish—including stingrays and other small sharks, even other hammerheads. These sharks sometimes travel in huge schools, which may include hundreds of individuals. That must be a spine-chilling sight, since this giant, on rare occasions, is known to attack humans.

Record Holder

The largest great hammerhead on record measured an astonishing 18 feet, 4 inches in length, and weighed 1,860 pounds.

THE GREAT WHITE SHARK

T HE MOST FEARED ANIMAL IN THE SEA IS PROBABLY THE GREAT WHITE SHARK. The largest of the meat-eating fish, the great white ranges in length from 10 feet to more than 20 feet. It regularly eats such large prey as sea lions, dolphins, turtles, and fish (including other sharks). Although equipped with a mouthful of saw-edged teeth, this shark doesn't rely on them to chew up a meal. Instead, it uses its up-to-3-inch-long shearing teeth to grip its prey while it bites off huge chunks of flesh. Smaller prey it simply swallows whole. Cruising continuously through the water at about two miles per hour, the 3,000-pound great white shark is capable of short bursts of speed of up to 25 miles per hour—or about ten times faster than a human swimmer.

Record Holder

The largest fish caught by rod and reel was a 3,388-pound, 16-foot-long great white shark caught in Brisbane, Australia. It took the fisherman nearly five hours to capture the powerful animal.

THE GREAT BARRACUDA

I N THE WARM WATERS OF THE CARIBBEAN SEA, THE GREAT BARRACUDA IS often as dreaded as the shark. This is due in part to the fact that the curious creature typically comes near human swimmers for a closer look and has reportedly attacked skin divers. The largest of the 20 or so types of barracuda, the frightening great barracuda is usually 4 to 6 feet long, although some as long as 8 feet have been sighted. The streamlined sea dweller weighs up to 100 pounds, and its sharp, heavy-duty teeth and powerful jaws are capable of biting other fish in half.

Fun Fact

The torpedo-shaped great barracuda attacks at lightning speed, swimming up to 27 miles per hour after its prey.

THE GIANT STARFISH

CAN YOU PICTURE A GIANT WITH FIVE ARMS, HUNDREDS OF FEET, AND NO head? This is the giant starfish of the Caribbean Sea, but don't let the name fool you. A starfish (also known as a sea star) is not a fish at all, but a type of creature called an echinoderm (ih-KY-nuh-derm). (This group of animals also includes sand dollars and sea urchins.) While some starfish are less than a fraction of an inch in size, the giant starfish stretches up to 20 inches from tip to tip. Using its five long arms that are lined with hundreds of tiny tube feet, this huge echinoderm moves slowly but surely over the rocky reefs that are its home. When it comes upon a clam or oyster to eat, the giant starfish uses the suckers at the end of its tube feet to pry open the shell.

Record Holder

In 1970 a starfish measuring 40 inches across and weighing about 11 pounds was discovered in the northern Pacific Ocean. By far, that's the largest starfish ever recorded.

THE OARFISH

T HE LONGEST OF THE BONY FISH, THE SNAKELIKE OARFISH MAY GROW TO AN amazing 30 feet or more and weigh 600 pounds. However, measurements of 10 feet long and 100 pounds are far more common. This toothless, scaleless fish is named for the lengthy, oar-shaped pelvic fins on its underside. Scientists know little about the daily life of the oarfish. It probably eats small fish and shrimp. Preferring fairly deep waters of 200 to 1000 feet, healthy adult fish are seldom seen. Young oarfish, however, are often found in the bellies of deep-water tuna.

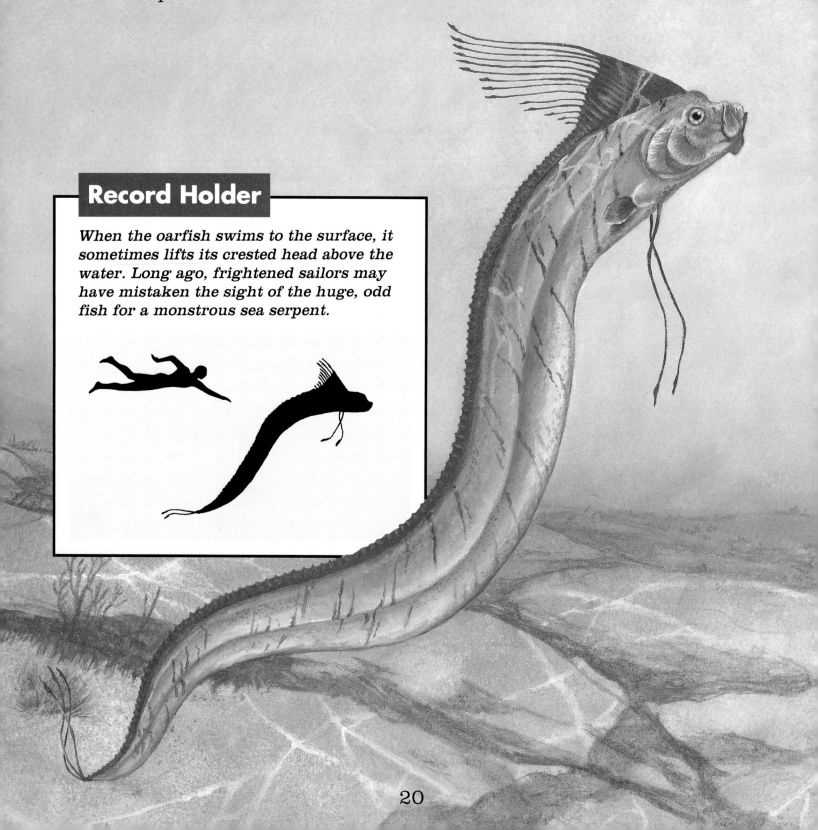

Record Holder

When the oarfish swims to the surface, it sometimes lifts its crested head above the water. Long ago, frightened sailors may have mistaken the sight of the huge, odd fish for a monstrous sea serpent.

THE SWORDFISH

AS ITS NAME IMPLIES, THIS COLOSSAL FISH IS EQUIPPED WITH A MOST UNUSUAL tool. Its long, flattened upper jaw forms a very effective bony sword that may extend up to 5 feet, or more than one-third of this mighty animal's 13-foot length. The 1,100-pound swordfish is toothless, but that doesn't seem to be a problem. When it sights a school of tasty fish or squid, the swordfish swims into the group and slashes left and right with its remarkable weapon. After stunning its prey in this way, the swordfish swallows them whole.

Fun Fact

A swordfish "sword" was once discovered embedded 2 feet deep in the wooden hull of a ship. For that to happen, the fish must have attacked the ship at a speed of about 40 miles per hour!

21

THE LEATHERBACK TURTLE

T HE LEATHERBACK TURTLE IS NOT ONLY THE LARGEST OF ALL LIVING TURTLES, but also the only sea turtle that does not have a hard shell. This great animal's smooth, leathery shell can be up to 5 feet long and the creature's overall length (including its head and tail) can be up to 8 feet long. The distance across its huge front flippers can sometimes measure 7 feet. The leatherback, which may weigh up to 1,500 pounds, has no teeth. It does have a sharp, powerful beak, however, which it uses to feed on jellyfish. This seagoing reptile is a great long-distance traveler and is known to swim the Atlantic Ocean all the way from the coast of South America to the shores of Canada.

Record Holder

The longest leatherback ever captured measured 9 feet long and 1,902 pounds.

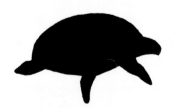

THE BLUEFIN TUNA

IF YOU WERE PUTTING TOGETHER A CATALOG OF FIERCE FISH, YOU MIGHT NOT think to include the tuna. Think again! Among the largest of the bony fish, the 14-foot-long, 2,000-pound bluefin tuna can be quite ferocious. This robust fish is a strong, swift swimmer. Schools of bluefin have been known to race at top speed into gatherings of smaller fish, ripping and tearing them to pieces. During such "feeding frenzies," the bluefin tuna destroy many more animals than they can possibly eat.

Record Holder

The fastest speed ever clocked for a bluefin tuna was 43.4 miles per hour. When racing through the water at such speeds, the bluefin lays its front fins into grooves along its body.

THE LION'S MANE JELLYFISH

SEEN ON THE SURFACE OF THE SEA, THE LION'S MANE JELLYFISH, THE LARGEST of the jellyfish, is a very impressive animal. Its float, or bell (its main body), may be as wide as 3 feet across. There is, however, more to this animal than meets the eye: Trailing down from the bell are pale yellow tentacles that can be 75 feet or more in length. This jellyfish captures the small fish it eats by stunning them with the powerful, stinging cells that line its wispy tentacles. When hunting, the creature sinks slowly, allowing its tentacles to spread in a wide, delicate net. Its great length allows the animal to cover a wide area and come in contact with a large number of prey.

Record Holder

The greatest size ever recorded for a lion's mane jellyfish was 7 ½ feet across the bell, with the animal's tentacles trailing to a length of 120 feet!

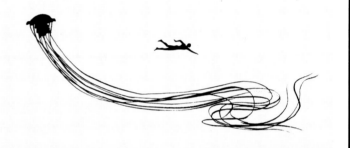

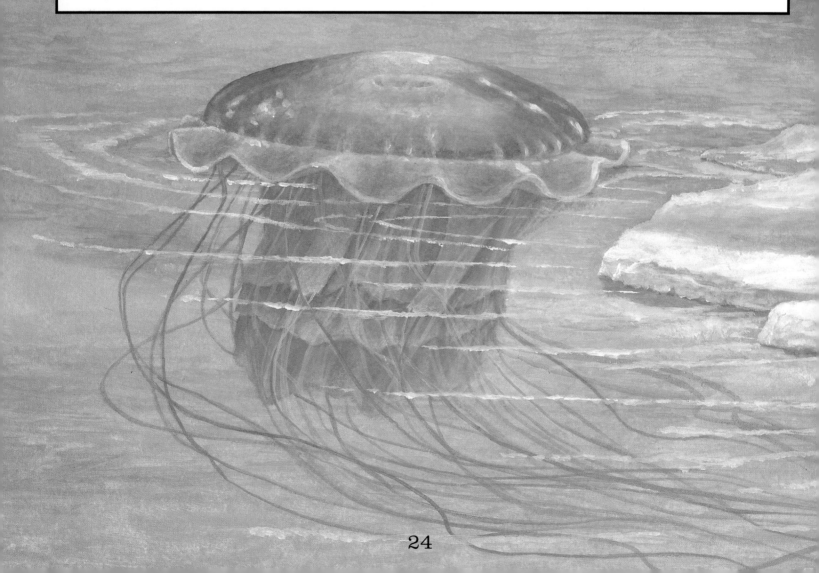

THE WALRUS

EVERYTHING ABOUT THIS NORTHERN GIANT IS SPECTACULAR. THE ROTUND body of a large male (called a bull) may reach up to 13 feet in length—about the same as an average car. Such a giant may tip the scales at well over 2,500 pounds. A female (or cow) is generally three-quarters the length and half the weight of a bull. The walrus has a 3- to 4-inch thick layer of blubber under its tough hide that keeps it warm in even the iciest water. This sea mammal also has a pair of sharp tusks that may be as long as 3 feet on a bull and 2 feet on a cow. These oversized teeth come in handy when the massive animal must pull itself up onto a slippery ice floe.

Fun Fact

During the breeding season, walruses gather in tremendous, noisy herds that may include more than 1,000 animals. The males battle for females, using their tusks as weapons.

THE HUMPBACK WHALE

T HE BLUE WHALE ISN'T THE ONLY GIANT WHALE THAT SWIMS IN ALL THE Earth's oceans. The humpback whale—weighing up to 100,000 pounds—is also found in deep waters worldwide. As with the blue whale, it is the female humpback that holds the size record. It is not unusual for a female humpback to be 50 feet long—as much as a locomotive! The humpback is a baleen whale. The sea mammal feeds daily on tons of tiny krill and fish that it strains from the water with its up to 700 bristly, black baleen plates. These plates are each up to 2 feet long. The male humpback is often called "the singing whale." Its beautiful calls are more varied and complex than those of any other whale.

Record Holder

At nearly 14 feet in length, the pectoral, or chest, fins of the humpback are the longest on any of the whales.

THE GRAY WHALE

THE BARNACLE-COVERED, 45-FOOT-LONG GRAY WHALE IS A FAMILIAR SIGHT off the western coast of the United States. It is one of the few gigantic whales to inhabit mainly coastal waters, which are easily reached by curious humans. The 72,000-pound gray whale doesn't always swim near the surface, though. It spends a great deal of its time feeding near the sea bottom. It searches for food by sucking mud into its mouth, then using its 300 baleen plates, each up to 15 inches long, to filter out tiny animals living in the mud. A layer of blubber 10 inches thick helps to keep this whale warm no matter what the water temperature.

Record Holder

The greatest migration of any mammal is the journey of the gray whale. Each year it treks along the Pacific coast—from Alaska to Baja and back again, a round-trip of some 12,000 miles.

THE WHALE SHARK

EVEN BOATS MAKE WAY FOR THE WHALE SHARK, WHICH CAN BE AS LONG AS 40 feet and weigh an astounding 30,000 to 40,000 pounds. At first glance you might mistake this creature for a whale, but its tall, crescent-shaped tail quickly identifies it as a fish—the world's largest. Although this animal's tremendous jaws are lined with hundreds of tiny, sharp teeth, it is a harmless filter feeder. It swims with its 6-foot-wide mouth open to gather plankton and small fish. You may not be surprised to hear that this gentle giant lays the largest eggs in the world. Because the foot-long eggs look like leather purses that women might carry, they are known as "mermaid's purses."

Record Holder

The largest known whale shark was captured in 1919. This animal was 60 feet, 9 inches long, and its weight was estimated at a staggering 80,000 pounds.

THE MEGAMOUTH SHARK

IN 1976, WHEN THE CREW MEMBERS OF A U.S. NAVY RESEARCH VESSEL IN Hawaii raised anchor, they got a big surprise. The first megamouth shark to be discovered by humans had become entangled in the lines. This shark, which was named for its huge, cavernous mouth, is known to reach nearly 15 feet in length, but much larger individuals may exist. It's hard to believe that such a huge creature could go unnoticed for so long, but the megamouth is thought to live in fairly deep water, between 1,000 and 2,000 feet below the surface. Although the jaws of the megamouth are lined with hooked teeth, this fish is a filter feeder.

Fun Fact

The silvery inner lining of this shark's mouth is dotted with round pores. Some scientists think that these pores may be light-producing organs that attract shrimp into the animal's gaping mouth.

THE BLUE MARLIN

THE BLUE MARLIN OF THE ATLANTIC OCEAN IS A MEMBER OF A FAMILY OF FISH that also includes the sailfish. These fish are known for their huge size and aggressive spirit, and that description certainly fits the Atlantic blue marlin. From tip to tip, this creature (on average) is as long as a rowboat (about 10 feet), and it can easily weigh 600 pounds or more. Because of its great size, this fish is able to hunt and feed on very large prey. One captured marlin had the remains of a 5-foot-long tuna in its belly. Despite this tremendous size, however, the marlin is swift, agile, and known for its spectacular leaps out of the water. In one jump, a blue marlin covered the distance of 130 feet—twice the length of a bowling alley!

Record Holder

The blue marlin's western cousin, the Pacific black marlin, is the largest and fastest of the marlins. It may reach 14 feet in length and weigh 1,500 pounds. Even over long distances, it can sustain speeds of up to 50 miles per hour.

THE SAILFISH

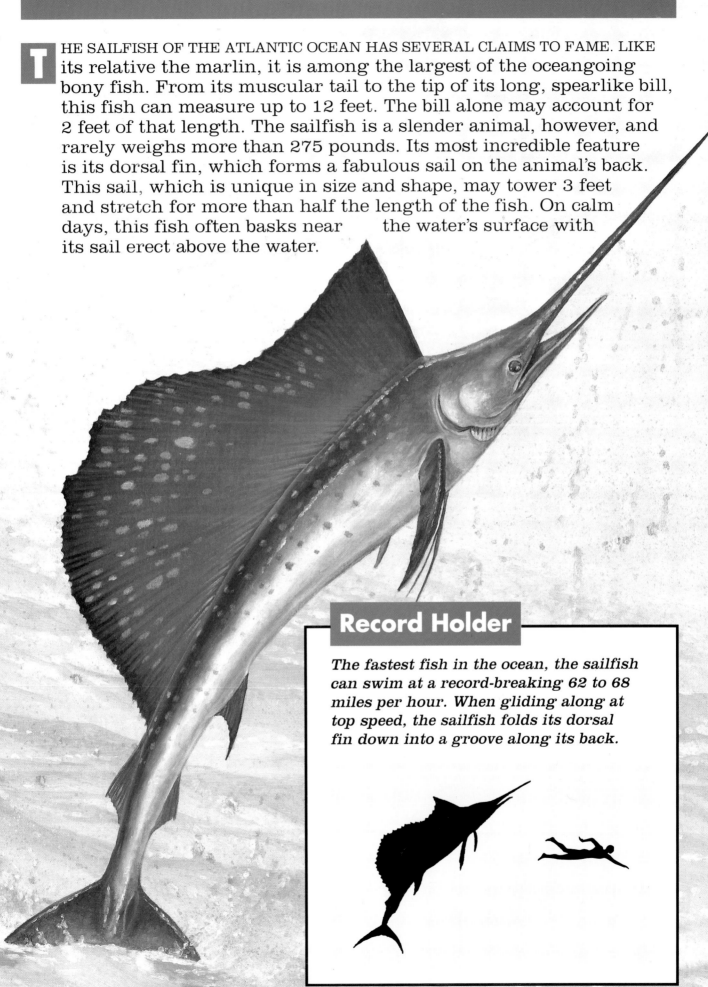

T HE SAILFISH OF THE ATLANTIC OCEAN HAS SEVERAL CLAIMS TO FAME. LIKE its relative the marlin, it is among the largest of the oceangoing bony fish. From its muscular tail to the tip of its long, spearlike bill, this fish can measure up to 12 feet. The bill alone may account for 2 feet of that length. The sailfish is a slender animal, however, and rarely weighs more than 275 pounds. Its most incredible feature is its dorsal fin, which forms a fabulous sail on the animal's back. This sail, which is unique in size and shape, may tower 3 feet and stretch for more than half the length of the fish. On calm days, this fish often basks near   the water's surface with its sail erect above the water.

Record Holder

The fastest fish in the ocean, the sailfish can swim at a record-breaking 62 to 68 miles per hour. When gliding along at top speed, the sailfish folds its dorsal fin down into a groove along its back.

THE KILLER WHALE

T HE KILLER WHALE, OR ORCA, IS NOT A WHALE AT ALL, BUT THE LARGEST member of the dolphin family. (Dolphins and whales are close relatives, but not members of the same animal family.) This up-to-30-foot-long, 18,000-pound giant is one of the only members of its family known to feed on warm-blooded animals, including other whales and dolphins. Killer whales are also called "wolves of the sea" because they swim in a "pack," or pod. A single pod of killer whales may include as many as 40 animals or as few as 3. Because of their size, these sea mammals are capable of some remarkable hunting tactics. Working together, they can actually lift and tip floating ice to slide prey, such as a seal, into the water.

Record Holder

The killer whale has the tallest dorsal fin of any sea mammal. You can tell the sex of this animal from the shape of this fin. A male's dorsal fin is straight and may rise up to 6 feet from the animal's back. A female has a shorter, curved fin.

THE LEOPARD SEAL

IKE ITS JUNGLE-DWELLING NAMESAKE, THE LEOPARD SEAL IS AN EXCELLENT hunter. This huge mammal is the only seal that regularly feeds on warm-blooded animals (as well as fish and squid). Its prey includes penguins and other seals, particularly the pups of the crabeater seal. The female leopard seal, which is slightly larger than the male, may be a little more than 13 feet long and weigh a hefty 840 pounds. Both male and female are equipped with curved, stabbing teeth. The size, speed, and fierceness of the leopard seal makes it one of Antarctica's most formidable predators.

Fun Fact

A leopard seal can easily leap from the water onto an ice floe 6 feet above the surface. To do this, the seal must be swimming at least 12 miles per hour, or nearly five times the swimming speed of an adult human.

THE ELEPHANT SEAL

T HE WORLD'S LARGEST LAND ANIMAL IS THE ELEPHANT, AND THE WORLD'S largest seal is the southern elephant seal. The male, or bull, southern elephant seal may be 20 feet long and weigh 8,000 pounds—nearly as long and as heavy as an Indian elephant. (The female, or cow, rarely grows to more than half that size.) The male also has a foot-long, trunklike snout, which he puffs up to boost the sound of his threatening roar. The great size of this sea mammal can sometimes be a sad disadvantage. During battles between bulls for mates, quarreling males (or even frightened females trying to get out of the way) can roll over and crush a baby. As many as one in five baby elephant seals die this way.

Fun Fact

The giant southern elephant seal may be quite clumsy on land, but in the water it is very graceful. It can dive to depths of more than 5,000 feet and remain underwater for up to 45 minutes.

THE EMPEROR PENGUIN

S IZE IS AN IMPORTANT REASON WHY THE EMPEROR PENGUIN IS WELL SUITED to its icy environment. Large animals do not lose body heat as quickly as small animals do and, at 5 feet tall and 90 pounds, the emperor is the largest of all the penguins. Its skin has a thick layer of blubber underneath and a tightly packed layer of tiny, waterproof feathers above. This arrangement keeps the huge bird warm in the frigid waters and protects it against the freezing cold Antarctic winter, when temperatures may drop to -80 degrees Fahrenheit.

Record Holder

The emperor penguin is the deepest-diving bird of any kind. It plunges to depths of more than 870 feet beneath the surface to feed on fish.

THE GREAT BARRIER REEF

THE GREAT BARRIER REEF STRETCHES FOR 1,250 MILES OFF THE COAST OF northeastern Australia. The largest living structure in the world, it is a vast collection of more than 2,000 individual reefs, and it occupies nearly 90,000 miles—an area about twice the size of the state of New York. The Great Barrier Reef is made of a thin layer of living coral polyps, which are tiny, soft-bodied sea creatures that each measure no more than a quarter of an inch across. Below the living coral is a huge nonliving core, which is composed of the stony skeletons of billions of coral polyps that have died. When the top, living layer dies off, a new one takes its place, and the reef grows outward and upward in linked colonies that may each include thousands of individuals. The Great Barrier Reef provides homes for thousands of species of living things, including sea snails, shrimp, sponges, starfish, crabs, and at least one-tenth of all known living species of fish.

Record Holder

The Great Barrier Reef is among the Earth's oldest living structures. The first phase of its growth began 20 million to 30 million years ago. Its most recent phase of growth began about 8,000 years ago.

THE GIANT CLAM

YOU MAY HAVE HEARD STORIES OF HUGE, MAN-EATING CLAMS SLAMMING SHUT on unsuspecting divers. Actually, the giant clam is an inoffensive animal that feeds on tiny creatures that it filters from seawater. Its three-foot-wide shell closes slowly enough that a diver would have to be very careless to get stuck. That's fortunate because reopening the shell of a closed 500-pound clam would take nearly 1,000 pounds of pressure. The average weight of this reef-dwelling mollusk is about 440 pounds. However, the soft, living creature inside the shell rarely weighs more than 25 pounds. The giant clam sometimes produces a giant pearl. Divers once discovered one that weighed an amazing 15 pounds.

Record Holder

The shell of the largest known giant clam is in the American Museum of Natural History in New York City. Found on Australia's Great Barrier Reef, the shell weighs 580 pounds and measures 43 inches across and 29 inches wide.

THE YELLOW SEA SNAKE

THE LONGEST OF THE SEA-DWELLING SNAKES IS THE YELLOW SEA SNAKE OF the South Pacific. Its average length is about 5 feet, but according to reliable reports individuals can grow to 9 feet. Like all sea snakes, this creature is an air breather and must surface regularly, but it seems to be able to remain submerged for an hour or more at a time. All sea snakes are venomous, and the yellow sea snake is no exception. This reptile delivers venom through its small fangs to subdue such prey as fish and shrimp. Although the venom is potent enough to kill a human, the yellow sea snake is generally not known to attack people.

Fun Fact

Like all sea snakes, the yellow sea snake may occasionally be bothered by small barnacles that attach themselves to the snake's skin. Fortunately, the problem is not permanent. The sea snake simply sheds the barnacles when it sheds its skin!

THE PACIFIC JEWFISH

GROUPERS ARE TYPICALLY LARGE FISH THAT ARE FOUND IN WARM WATERS worldwide. The giant among these heavy-bodied sea creatures is the Pacific jewfish. Also known as the Queensland grouper, this fish may reach a length of 12 feet and weigh up to 800 pounds. When hunting smaller fish, the Pacific jewfish lurks quietly in ambush, sheltered by rock or coral. As its prey comes within reach, the huge fish suddenly sucks in water, victim and all. Although this fish is not known to bother humans, divers claim to have been followed by large Pacific jewfish. Reportedly, the aggressive giants will charge menacingly if a diver ventures too close.

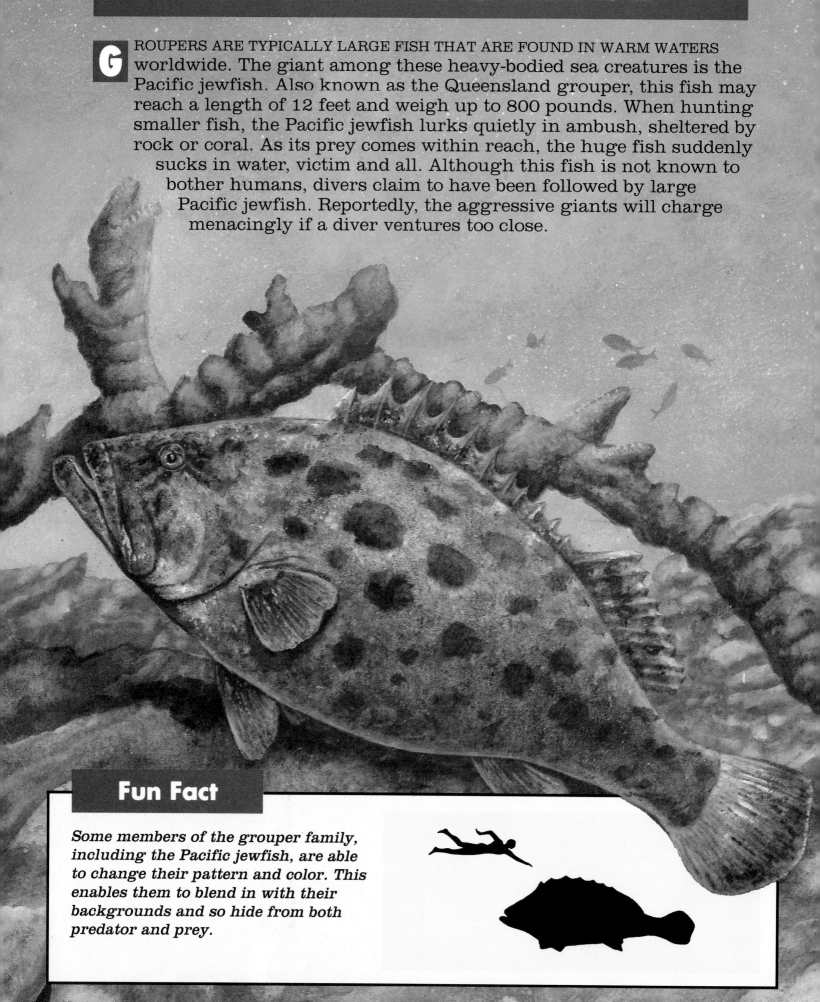

Fun Fact

Some members of the grouper family, including the Pacific jewfish, are able to change their pattern and color. This enables them to blend in with their backgrounds and so hide from both predator and prey.

THE AUSTRALIAN TRUMPET

THE WORLD'S LARGEST SHELLED SNAIL ACTUALLY LIVES IN THE SEA AND breathes through gills. It is the Australian trumpet. This animal glides slowly across the Great Barrier Reef of Australia on a single rubbery "foot." Wherever it goes, the Australian trumpet carries its beautiful 2-foot-long, 5-pound shell with it. When threatened, the snail can withdraw safely into this hard, protective shell. The Australian trumpet is a meat eater, feeding on slow-moving snails and clams. It laps (or licks) at its prey with a raspy tonguelike organ called a radula (RAD-yoo-luh). The radula is lined with extremely tiny teeth that scrape up food and carry it into the snail's mouth.

Record Holder

The smallest snail in the sea is a mere $\frac{1}{37}$th-of-an-inch long. It lives between sand grains on the beaches of certain Japanese islands. The Australian trumpet is more than 800 times longer than this mini-snail!

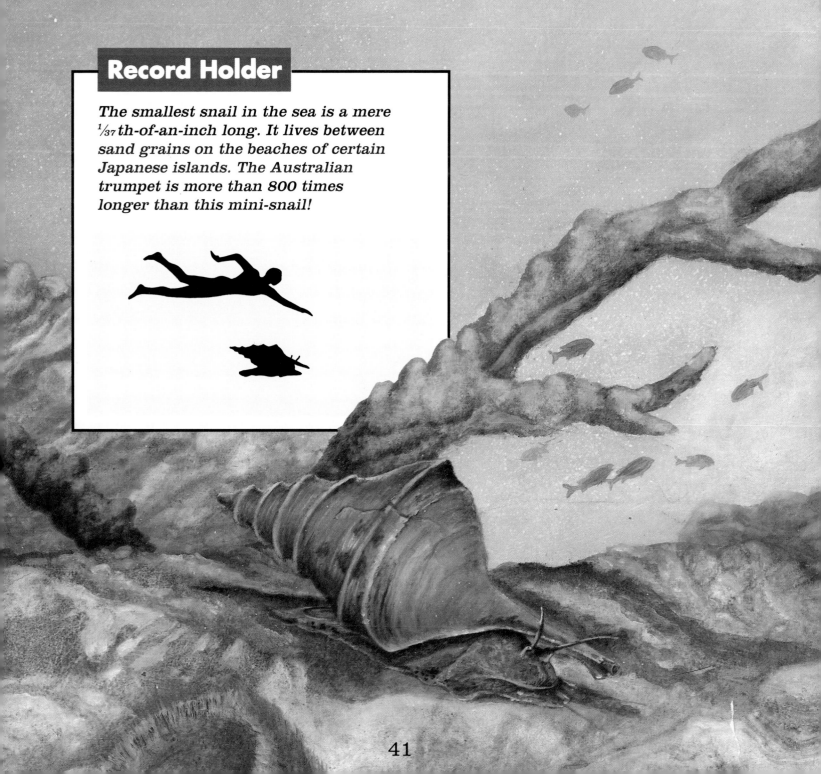

THE JAPANESE SPIDER CRAB

THE DEEP WATERS OFF THE COAST OF JAPAN ARE HOME TO THE GIANT Japanese spider crab, the largest of all crabs—indeed, the largest of all arthropods (a category of animals that includes crabs, lobsters, spiders, and insects). Also called the stilt crab, this animal has a pear-shaped body that is about 1 foot long, and it weighs an average of 20 pounds. The distance from tip to tip of this amazing animal's out-stretched claws is an incredible 12 feet or more. Scrambling across the muddy sea bottom, this spindly crab scavenges the flesh of dead fish or anything else that it can find.

Record Holder

The largest Japanese spider crab ever discovered was said to have been double the average weight, and its claws spanned nearly 19 feet!

THE GIANT SEA ANEMONE

THE GIANT SEA ANEMONE (uh-NEM-uh-nee) LIVES AMONG THE REEFS OF THE warm waters of the eastern Pacific Ocean. The largest of the anemones, this simple animal looks like a huge flower. Its body is basically a long tube with a disk at one end that enables the creature to attach itself securely to a reef. At the other end of the tube is the animal's mouth, which is surrounded by a wide ring of tentacles. This ring may be as much as 3 feet across. When the anemone is feeding, it stretches out its 8-foot-long tentacles to catch small crabs, shrimp, and fish. Stinging cells in these tentacles paralyze the prey, which is then brought toward the anemone's mouth. When it is touched, the giant anemone can rapidly withdraw its tentacles and close in on itself, which helps it avoid having its tentacles nibbled upon by predators.

Fun Fact

Unlike most fish, the tiny 2- to 5-inch-long clownfish swims safely among the tentacles of the giant anemone. The relationship benefits both animals. The colorful fish attracts larger prey to within reach of the anemone's stinging tentacles. The tentacles protect the clownfish from these predators and also allow it to feed on scraps the anemone leaves behind.

THE ELECTRIC EEL

T HE WORLD'S OCEANS AREN'T THE ONLY PLACE TO DISCOVER GIANTS WITH fins. Impressively large creatures also swim in fresh waters. The Amazon River is where you will find the electric eel. This fish, which grows up to 8 feet long and weighs 50 pounds, generates electricity in special organs in its tail. These organs take up more than three-quarters of the animal's length and are made up of columns of tiny, thin cells. A large electric eel may have a million or more of these cells. The electric eel can use low levels of electricity to signal to others of its kind, or full power to defend itself. The unusual fish can even generate enough power to kill a human swimmer up to 10 feet away. Not surprisingly, this Amazon dweller has few natural enemies.

Record Holder

The largest South American electric eel yet to be discovered weighed about 90 pounds. Its electric organs made up approximately half of the animal's weight.

44

THE ARAPAIMA

I T'S EASY TO SEE WHY THE HUGE ARAPAIMA (air-uh-PY-muh) WAS ONCE AN important food source for Indians living along the banks of the Amazon River. The largest fish of the Amazon, the arapaima, also called the pirarucu (peer-uh-ROO-koo), measures nearly 8 feet in length and can weigh 300 pounds. An efficient hunter, it feeds on other fish. Instead of taking in oxygen from the water, this unusual giant breathes air at the surface. Adults usually come to the surface every 15 minutes or so to gulp air noisily. When the water level rises during the rainy season, the female arapaima hollows out an 8-inch-deep nest in the muddy river bottom and deposits between 40,000 and 50,000 eggs.

Fun Fact

To the South American Indians living along the Amazon River, every part of the arapaima was once considered valuable. At one time, the Indians even used the dried flesh of this huge fish as currency.